W0007663

FOREWORD

Being a professional musician in the 21st century has never been more exciting with the abundance of resources and materials available for us to consult in order to better our overall work. Because of the wealth of materials that are openly accessible to us, we are fortunate to be able to share ideas, think critically, and develop our characters as musicians, teachers, and people as a whole.

...so of all of the materials available everywhere, why this book?

I still remember picking up Kristin's first book, How I Made $100,000 My First Year as a Piano Teacher, and reading it cover to cover without putting it down. As an undergraduate student at The University of Southern California, I wanted to learn beyond what the classroom taught me, and so I read every pedagogical and business-related book I could get my hands on. Even then, and still, Kristin's book stands out as one of the most impactful pieces of literature I read in establishing my own successful piano studio (Regina's Music Studio in South Pasadena.) I am fortunate enough to be able to call Kristin not only a brilliant influence in my career, but also my friend.

The Mindset of a $100,000 Piano Teacher nails the concept of focusing on your growth mindset to translate through your teaching and daily lifestyle. This book provides a pathway that will help you integrate all of the modern tools of the 21st century into making your studio as successful as it can possibly be.

I wish you happy reading, dear teacher, and hope you will gain as much as I did from Kristin's books!

Regina Ngo, Owner of Regina's Music Studio, Los Angeles, CA

PREFACE

Why music?

Living as a professional musician is so much more than playing an instrument on a high level. What made you decide to pursue music professionally? Was there a moment, an experience or person who inspired and pushed you? When I reflect and work to articulate my "why," it goes back to achievement. I was always working to achieve and improve internally. My goal is always to keep growing.

I love being a teacher of music. I love to hear, see and feel growth in myself as well as my students. And? I'm good at it. I'm genuinely interested in my students, and I enjoy helping them achieve their musical goals. It really is as simple as this: I teach because I love to see growth. Growth, though, is a funny thing because I would guess that if we had fifteen people in a room, we would have fifteen different (passionate) responses about what growth looks like.

When I speak of growth, I'm not limiting myself or students to a level or acquisition of particular skills. In my mind growth is simple. It's the point of moving forward and evolving to be better today than we were yesterday. The question I continually ask is how do I evolve into my best self and what can I do for my students that allows them to be their best selves. What's great today needs to be better tomorrow, and in each season of our lives growth looks just a bit different, doesn't it? Sometimes being great is simply being happy, or feeling fulfilled. Sometimes it's this state of flow where everything comes together and just works. And sometimes it means we are in a period of change and challenge.

My personal metrics for growth that remain consistent in each season of life include the enjoyment factor, sense of accomplishment and ability to demonstrate grit and persevere through whatever it is I am working on. If I am at all gritty, then I know I am committed and interested.

I would be remiss if I told you everything was always rosy and forward-moving, especially when I face the artist's dilemma of "what's next." It's through the periods of challenge and frustration where I grow the most. Consistent reinvention of one's self and one's musical and teaching craft is the key to success and longevity as an artist. Teaching artists are keenly aware of the absolute need to keep themselves and their teaching fresh. If you are a teacher who does the same thing year after year, I challenge you to tap into your inner creative instincts.

What better opportunity do we have to fail forward (and grow) than through music? Every single time we learn a new piece of music, or want to learn something by ear, we have to start at (relatively) ground zero. That's a whole lot of mental strength.

Another reason to love teaching music is because of the opportunity to give back to community. I feel fulfilled in being able to provide a service to people who I know will benefit mentally, emotionally and, for some, spiritually, by studying music. I love seeing and hearing my students perform well; from a solid recital performance or adjudicated event performances to working toward achieving a higher score on their Royal Conservatory exam, it's personally gratifying to be able to elevate other people. I also love seeing students play music they enjoy and making that music come to life. Seeing the joy on family members' faces when their children or grandchildren perform well is also uplifting. See where I'm going with this? I *love* what I do.

We all have goals. Some of us are better at reflection and writing them down, following up, and so on, but we all have them. My primary goal for teaching is different than my daily motivation of continual growth, though they are linked. It's a little bit science and a little bit art. As a teaching artist, my end goal as I see it is that I want my students to support live music when they have the opportunities as an adult. I want them to *feel* fulfilled throughout their musical journey. Music lessons, if I am doing them right, should not simply be a discipline or checking of a box. It's not just about replicating someone else's ideas. I want to see each student carry on music learning with their children, and for their lives to be more fulfilled from their time learning music with me and at my school. It is my hope that each of my students flourish in their lives and discover what it feels like to be passionate. The primary passion in life for one of your students could be bugs. It could be running, art, football, science or politics. When you have passion, you have so much potential for growth, which spreads joy and accomplishment and leads people to healthier, more fulfilled lives. It's simple: through enough grit or perseverance, anything then becomes possible.

Living fully

Making music and sharing my love of it is the one thing I have been consistent about throughout my life. I love the process of creating, learning, feeling good about what I am doing and being able to give to others. I go in and out of other interests, but music is always present, and education/helping others at the forefront.

The inspiration for writing this book comes from a desire to reach other musicians and teaching artists who want to genuinely live their life fully, consistently and with intention that recognizes evolution and creativity as core to who we are. I wish I would have had this information when I was earning my degrees. The school of life and hard knocks taught me the majority of what I know and what works in operating a music business. As independent artists, it's a challenge sometimes to find your tribe and be part of something bigger. It's easy for us to want to go at things alone, because that's what we do regularly. Through the internet and reading, I have amassed so much valuable information; what you will read here is just the tip of the iceberg to get you started.

I want to share with you what has worked for me to streamline processes and have peace of mind in financial matters, so that we can all be fully present and thrive in this world. As a teaching artist, your goals are probably similar to mine: to *experience* joy, *feel* a sense of accomplishment, have a *desire* to grow forward and be able to realize a wide range of emotions from joy to sadness and peace and beyond.

With these goals in mind, we need to be able to automate the parts of our lives that drain our energy. Teaching artists need to be able to communicate and reach people at levels we didn't realize were possible. Our impact has the potential to transform an entire community that can go on and pay it forward by impacting their new communities. In this book, I am going to share with you what has given me peace of mind in running a successful home studio as well as music school. You will receive a detailed roadmap that has a proven track record, and a list of some of the best books out there, in my opinion. This will either act as a springboard for further study, or at the very least lead you to make improvements and help you reach a better state of flow in your business.

To live one's life fully and reach a place of contentment and growth, we need to create and implement a big-think, long-view vision for ourselves. Who wants to be the musician working for a ridiculously low wage, always feeling disgruntled, jaded by the profession and not be

The Mindset of a $100,000 Piano Teacher

able to retire? I most certainly don't. I want the *option* of retirement with peace of mind at 60, or earlier. Now is the time to set ourselves up to implement a long-view strategy that lays the groundwork for a life fully lived. Now is the time to set ourselves up for financial success, which *is* possible as an independent teaching artist. The biggest ideas take small, consistent steps, which is where the hard, sometimes monotonous and potentially not-fun work comes in. This book sets out to help you through the process of transformation and evolution into your best self, wherever that may take you.

Before we get started, I recommend you make a list of your personal strengths and weaknesses. Then, ask yourself how you can do more of the strengths to sharpen those skills, and less of the things at which you don't excel. Choose three strengths and three weaknesses. As an example: I'm not good at calling people back on the phone. It's an inefficient use of my time and it drains my energy, so I hired an assistant to handle the phone. She *likes* doing that, which means that we both win. I can then spend my time pursuing, actively engaging in and sharpening my skills to be an expert in other areas of my business.

Here's another example: I want to be an expert teacher. Teacher of what you ask? Teacher of children. Teacher of adults. Teacher of teachers. All of it. I have a lot of work to do. This is why I don't have time to answer the phone. Focus and develop your strengths and work to hire others to do the work you aren't good at and don't really have an interest in improving. I have a day-to-day accountant for a reason. It's not that I can't, it's that I am inconsistent and I want things done right, and on time.

What is a teaching artist?

A teaching artist is a term that came about sometime in the 1970s out of a reaction to a less than desirable term: "resource professional." This was used to describe activities of artists in schools, which sounds clinical and anything but creative. June Dunbar at Lincoln Center Institute is attributed with the change in term.

The term teaching artist is broader and more descriptive than, simply, teacher. When you add the second word, artist, it gives a whole new meaning to what a teacher is and does. One of my favorite ways to describe it comes from Eric Booth's *Music Teaching Artist's Bible*: "Teaching artistry is the artful, effective, engaging, successful, joyful, transformative, proven way to guide humans into and through those experiences." If you don't own Booth's book already, I cannot recommend it highly enough. For this book, I hope to show you how I have personally thrived and provided musical experiences that I believe are artful, effective, engaging, joyful and transformative.

What exactly does it mean to thrive?

To thrive means to develop vigorously or to flourish. Thriving is a mental space that you start with, which you turn into physical action that makes *you* develop and flourish from the inside. Always being beholden to others emotions, ideas and ways of being is not being true to who we are. The mirror is a great thing. When we study ourselves, the mirror teaches us what we need to be spending our time working on. I need to spend some time focusing on what I really want, what I am feeling and what my intentions are going into any situation. To thrive is the internal way we approach and live our lives on a daily basis. Are you inspired every day? Most days? If you aren't looking forward to each day as a teaching artist, what is it that you need to change in order to get there? This book explores what makes our lives as teaching artists more valuable, less cumbersome and gives ideas for raising your earning potential as a music teaching artist.

If you're still with me, let's go ahead and get started.

CHAPTER 1
DEEP WORK: REFLECT AND SLOW DOWN

- Musicality for artful living
- Seeing our students as a collection of strengths, not of weaknesses
- Mastery, Purpose and Autonomy = Keys to Flourishing

"Deep Work" is the internal, focused work that delves into your inner world. You know, that place where you spend most of your time. Deep work is a period of time you set aside to train your mind to go into the depths of your soul that daily life oftentimes doesn't allow. When we are engaged in deep work, feelings and emotions that we didn't even know existed all of a sudden come flooding to the surface. Think prayer, meditation, yoga, journaling, etc...every day.

Deep work is a challenge for me. It's a time when one must embrace boredom. Turn off the social media, turn off the TV, put the phone in airplane mode and simply just "be." When I set out and work on deep work intentions, some of my best ideas and realizations come to fruition.

I start my day with thirty minutes of nonsocial media-based reading, a walk with my dog, plus 30 to 60 minutes of exercise, a good cup (or two) of strong coffee and, at minimum, one weekly written reflection. What really unsettles me is when I am not focused, when I float from one thing to another without deciding on a real plan for forward motion. Floating without intention makes me feel as if I am leading an aimless existence, as if I am relying more on chance happenings than a plan. This is, for me, a recipe for anxiety.

Living life fully is about doing what you love on a daily basis, where you can't imagine doing anything else. If you are not careful, running your music studio or school will take control of your schedule, your thoughts and will burn you out.

Over the last ten years, I have reached periods where I felt burned out. In order to recover and regain energy, I needed to carve out large chunks of time for open space. There were days when I didn't feel like doing what I needed to do, days when I simply didn't feel like working on my business. Some days I didn't even feel like teaching.

Mel Robbins wrote this great book, which I recommend you purchase. It's called *The 5 Second Rule,* which basically says that whatever you need to do, or desire to do but lack the motivation to get it done, just count backward from 5: 5-4-3-2-1, and then do whatever it is you're gearing up to do. As artists, it's difficult for us to detach how we *feel* about ourselves, but it's necessary. We are the only ones that can hold ourselves accountable and we give way too much power to our feelings.

Another favorite book of mine about getting things done is *The War of Art* by Steven Pressfield. He writes about the barriers and obstacles we put up that keep us from doing what we say. He says all we need is consistent, creative discipline. Big, grandiose ideas are great, but they go nowhere without creative discipline.

Let's talk about musicality as a metaphor for artful living for a moment. Musicality is broad and encompasses a lot of nuance. Wikipedia defines it this way: "sensitivity to, knowledge of, or talent for music," or, "the quality or state of being musical." The Oxford Dictionary says musicality is "musical talent or sensitivity" with some examples such as "her beautiful, rich tone and innate musicality."

Musicality at Musical-U.com is described as "a set of 'inner skills' which let you freely and confidently express yourself in music." That in itself is a partial truth, because somewhere along the line of learning someone taught the performer (at least some of) those "inner skills." Some of the skills Musical-U believes are important are: playing by ear, singing in tune, jamming, having good rhythm, writing music, improvising a solo, reading notation, playing from a lead sheet, performing live and playing multiple instruments.

If we use musicality as a metaphor for artful living, we can make parallels such as being open-minded, self-aware, having the ability and freedom to experience fun, generate new ideas (being creative), spending time being well-read and interested in multiple subjects/having hobbies. When we isolate, stay stuck in our ways and avoid new experiences, we limit ourselves, preventing us from truly thriving. Thriving does not happen in a box. Thriving happens when you live intentionally. It's authentic.

Where am I going with this, you ask? To be artful and capable of a full life, we must first be aware and have an open mind to explore what it is that excites us. We must have the discipline and grit to reinvent our teaching and ourselves, using new ideas that evolve into innovation. That said, there is a certain amount of discipline that must take place to achieve this. Just like in a music performance, there is an element of discipline in the practice room that leads us to our success on stage and, by extension, in our lives.

Seeing students as collections of strengths, rather than weaknesses

I am passionate about the strength and growth lenses through which we view our own lives, as well as our students. Focusing on our own personal strengths as well as the strengths of others is a fantastic way to reach inner peace and help others be their best selves.

With classical music in particular, it seems like we are hypercritical of everyone and how they approach everything. "Kristin can't play her way out of a paper bag" is something I might have heard from one of my advisors in graduate school. Or, "Todd's recital could have been so much better. He just isn't that musical."

I'd like to throw that toxicity out the window and see our profession flip that negative mindset to one of encouragement where we continually grow, do better and rise to our best selves. I see a lot of jazz musicians doing this. Seeing the world through a positive lens doesn't mean ignoring areas of improvement. Rather, it simply changes the *perception* of the individual and situation. It changes our inner voice too, which is the most important voice we have. Imagine if you started to think only of the good things, looking at life's experiences as an opportunity. It's a much more peaceful place!

A book I was highly influenced by is Carol Dweck's *Mindset: The New Psychology of Success.* Dweck talks about a fixed versus growth mindset in children and how we can use language to encourage our students (and ourselves) to be more growth minded.

Let's take a moment to reflect. Do you see yourself and your students as a collection of strengths or a collection of weaknesses? Just because people learn differently, or have a different value system, doesn't mean they are less than, not as talented or won't work as hard. It simply means these students are here to teach you and help you see the world in a different way.

One of my professors at the University of Wisconsin-Eau Claire has a daughter with Down syndrome. One day he was talking to a small group of us and telling us how much he loved his daughter and how much she has taught him. "You know, she really has life figured out. She sees everything and everyone as an opportunity and has so much inner joy," he said. Someone whom I might look at with pity or sadness is actually smarter than me. She gets life. She is the one who is thriving.

One of my favorite images on the internet is a picture of a tree with the following text: "For a fair selection, everybody has to take the same exam: Please climb that tree." Also in the image are a monkey, an elephant, a penguin, a fish in a bowl and a dog, with a man sitting behind a desk, administering the test. If we expect each learner to be exactly the same, we are setting our students and ourselves up for complete failure. As this popular quotation notes, "Everybody is a genius. But if you judge a fish by its ability to climb a tree, it will live its whole life believing that it is stupid." Sometimes it's more important to be uplifting than it is to be honest. Or maybe being uplifting is a form of honesty and we're choosing our words to affect the person.

I have a student who has been with me for approximately seven years, and it was in year six — after consistent, small steps — that we were able to get to the point of reading at a 2B level. Seven years. I tried everything, including color coding, until I learned he was color blind (that would have been helpful to know in the first month of my "colorful" efforts). The intriguing part of how he learns though, is that he can memorize anything you show him within the late elementary/early intermediate levels, and memorize it almost instantly. So, our lessons consist of both leaning into his strengths as well as reading, to which he tells me he is allergic. On the one hand, it is easy to be embarrassed as a teacher when a student can only read at a 2B level after seven years. On the other hand, he is making music, even reading music, he participates in talent shows at his school and clearly is proud of his achievements so far. He is bright, kind and has a huge heart. He attends his lessons every week. I am confident that he would have stopped playing piano if he would have had a teacher who saw him as a collection of weaknesses instead of the strengths that are uniquely his.

I see teachers evaluating students regularly with metrics that lack intention and with words that cut down instead of uplift. We see these wonderful humans thirty or forty-five minutes a week. We should ask ourselves, "what should be the most important thing they walk away with?" Who says it's important to play a Baroque piece at a high level in the third level of a method book? Who says each student should learn the same music at the same age? And if they don't, does that mean "they can't play their way out of a paper bag?" No, of course not. I see parents placing the same type of metric on their children. The science seems to have prevailed over the art, but it is *through* art that we reach our students and help them be their best selves.

Worried about those flat pinkies? Don't waste your energy. Keep working toward better shapes, but remember that sometimes things just work themselves out over time.

I now give to all of my graduating seniors a piece of art created by my friend Misty Oliver Foster that says, "Enjoy the Process." I love the message because the process is what learning is all about, not the end goal. The end goal of life is death, so why not enjoy everything to the best of our ability and grow from whatever experience life gives us? Spend the time focusing on what is going well with your students and work to improve the things that need it. Be honest. Be kind. And do these things consistently, methodically and patiently.

The Mindset of a $100,000 Piano Teacher

One of the areas that really gets me frustrated in piano study is arbitrary goals for repertoire and technique. For example, if a 4th grade student isn't playing music in A-flat, why are they learning the scale and triads for A-flat? The question we should always ask is, "Is what I am teaching today relevant for tomorrow?" If a student is a hobby learner who doesn't like practicing, but who values playing songs she really loves, why on earth would you intentionally choose music that she doesn't know? Why would you recommend this child to take an exam? In my opinion, simply "because it's good for them," is not a good enough reason. What will they learn and take away from this experience? Will it get them closer to *their* goals? Will they quit while you are working on *your* goals, and *your* mission? What is it about a piece of music they dislike that is important for them to learn? It's definitely more work to meet the student where they are, but so much more valuable.

Frequently, I am asked about what I think of teaching simplified arrangements of larger standard classical works (such as, "Fur Elise".) My rule of thumb is, if it's getting a student closer to the student's goals, they are making music and having fun, then why would you not?

The most motivating elements we have available to us to influence and positively affect our students are helping them achieve joy and mastery (or at the very least, a level of competency), giving each student a purpose or reason for doing, and encouraging the autonomy to flourish on their own, with their own voice.

Mastery, Purpose and Autonomy

People need autonomy. We all need purpose and levels of mastery in our lives in order to thrive. Purpose and autonomy need to be present for successful lessons, and for some teachers and students, so does mastery. For others, a hobby approach works just fine. Kind of like me and downhill skiing. I always have the "pizza move" to fall back on.

When I've taken lessons, I lose interest if my teacher is too technical. If she critiques me more than we "play," I won't want to continue lessons. Let's add some salsa dancing in this scenario too. I want to dance, while learning some pointers and vocabulary along the way. I also don't want to enter any competitions or performances. I want an experience. Each time I salsa dance or ski, I want to feel joy and feel ever so slightly challenged and accomplish something. Our students are likely in a similar boat. They want to grow, they want to play and they want to make their dreams to make music a reality. What new instrument or skill have you acquired or pursued recently where you were a beginner? How did it make you feel, and what did it do for your teaching?

Mastery: Mastery is comprehensive knowledge or a skill in a subject or accomplishment. Angela Duckworth writes in her book *Grit: The Power of Passion and Perseverence*, that Talent x Effort = Skill (mastery.) And that Skill x Effort = Achievement. We have to be good, and feel confident about our craft. There are so many levels of mastery, I'll let you determine which level is important to you and your students. As a reference point, for my students to pass a piece of music, my mastery number is 85/90 percent. On what level does one achieve "mastery" as a music teaching artist, or musician in general? What is the goal for each of your students?

Purpose: Purpose is the reason for which something is done or created, or for which something exists. It's why you get out of bed in the morning. Your reasons for doing.

Autonomy: Autonomy is freedom from external control or influence. It's another way to say independence. Autonomy will likely increase engagement over compliance. Isn't that a goal of the teaching artist?

Study after study leads to the same conclusion: workplace autonomy is the number one factor in whether a high value employee stays or goes.

The goal for us as teaching artists is usually to help our students achieve autonomy in their lessons, but what if our goal were to help them achieve autonomy in their musical journey? What if each of our students could play in a chamber group, or play for a retirement center and play music the residents really enjoyed? The ideas are different. Many of us tend to teach to the instrument, the piece or to the competition, rather than teaching for the broader goals of literacy, competency and enjoyment. Both are desirable in the market, and both have their place in our profession.

CHAPTER 2
BIG IDEAS, SMALL STEPS

1. Revolution v. Evolution

2. Creative Performance Ideas

3. Value of Current Music

4. Online Learning Opportunities

These are the four pillars that have defined the Centre for Musical Minds and my teaching style for the past ten years. Do you have your own pillars? If so, what are they and how have they set up your teaching approach? Each of these ideas helped me create the curriculum for my school as well as provide content for workshops I have been privileged to give around the United States, Germany and Hungary.

Evolution v. Revolution

The evolution of anything is the natural progression of what's next. A revolution is something that shakes things up. It's a dramatic, wide-reaching change.

A simple example of evolution is what happens after college graduation: you start your own teaching practice and implement some of what you learned and infuse a few original ideas of your own. A revolution is creating a studio or school that completely shakes things up for you, for your community and possibly the profession. Pedagogically, the most revolutionary teaching tool has been the invention and incorporation of the iPad in how children learn. In my experience, the children who use the iPad extensively are almost all purely discovery-based learners and treat learning like a video game.

The pop showcase recitals I started ten years ago (even before the brick and mortar CMM was running) were revolutionary at the time. Incorporating popular music in my teaching was evolutionary, but how I taught it was somewhat revolutionary, at least to me personally, because I created the path based on zero education and minimal experience. Figuring out how to effectively create and develop young artists using popular music has been one of the most exciting parts of my career.

Creative Performance Ideas

It's imperative we give our clients experience-based learning as well as meaningful performance experiences. Simply having traditional recitals isn't any more enjoyable to me than seeing a trained monkey going on stage and performing tricks. It's cute, sometimes impressive. But what value is being shared? The majority of my students would prefer not to participate in recitals, but they seem to look forward to our living room concerts, low-key and low-stress situations where playing for each other is about sharing instead of performing. We're artists and we're supposed to be creative and these traditional recitals are the best we have to offer?

I have been putting on a Pop Showcase for nine years, where I hire a rhythm section to play with our students. The first few years were phenomenal, and the concerts became increasingly better and smoother for about six years. But recently, this last year in fact, I found myself bored to tears by it. I sat there listening to familiar music and all I could think was, "Is this all there is?" It's not a good place to be, but it is an opportunity to grow. There was absolutely nothing new or innovative about it anymore. The kids played their pop song, many wrote their chord charts, and that was that. It was great and fun and new for the first couple years, but now I feel like it's the "same old, same old" and needs a facelift.

So what's next, you ask? I'm so glad you asked, because I have been thinking long and hard about that. This next spring we'll give our Pop Showcase a theme, perhaps a decade and genre, like Jazz and Blues, or 90's Music. We'll definitely add an MC and audience participation with awards. This is an example of evolution. The time has come to implement something different. The original idea however, is what I would consider revolutionary as a piano recital from a primarily classical teacher.

Performance experiences need to be an event to which students look forward. This means that not all recitals and performances should be on a stage where a child is asked to "prove themselves" in the traditional format. Whether that's how you view it or not, that's usually how kids see a recital. Am I against the traditional recital format? No. Do I think we can add more value by getting away from it and trying new things? Yes.

Here is a list of performance opportunities that I have personally tried and that worked well for my students and families enrolled at CMM.

- Themed performance classes
- Student-only performances
- Small living room concerts
- Chamber music (not just classical)
- Multi-instrument performances
- "Gigs" with song lists for volunteering at nursing homes, restaurants and business grand openings

- Family Music! Incorporating the whole family in a performance

Value of Current Music

I vividly remember a conversation in the lobby of the Westin Hotel in Lombard, Illinois at the National Conference on Keyboard Pedagogy, probably in 2009. The heated exchange was about what motivates children to keep pursuing music. I was stupefied at how backward I thought the person I was talking to had his priorities about teaching. Typical ivory tower mentality, if you will.

My friend was arguing that when the teacher is excited about a piece or style of music, this excitement then transfers to the student and they too become excited no matter what it is they play. On one level, I agree that it works for some students, sometimes, but it's not a good long-term plan or healthy view of what we can accomplish in private music lessons. We were talking about baroque and classical music for beginning students. I had strong feelings and opinions about a local festival that seemed dated to me and I thought it was silly to require a baroque piece so early on. My students checked the baroque box, but didn't enjoy it at all. My response to him was a question. Why is it important for a second or third grader who clearly is a hobby learner, to play a baroque piece and a sonatina for the Dallas Music Teachers Association Achievement Audition? If he is in his first few years of study, where should we be putting our energy? Polishing and performing these types of pieces takes a significant amount of time and level of perfection that even Horowitz would likely not get a I+ on. Who said this was important? *Why* is this important? Simply "because it's tradition" isn't good enough for me, and shouldn't be good enough for you.

We've been plodding along for decades with this "well-balanced diet," and yet all the research for longevity in music lessons points to less baroque and more of the familiar. I'm not saying baroque music and sonatinas are not important, at all. In fact, I love sonatinas and so do most of my students who are at an intermediate level, when they have a firm grasp on the technical elements required to play these pieces. My point in the discussion, which was the first time I had outwardly expressed my frustration, was that I wanted to excite my students on their individual music learning journey, and those boring old requirements were not an effective way. It's like taking a 6 hour detour on boring roads over a 36 hour long car trip that is otherwise pleasant and inspiring. It doesn't make any sense. Have Achievement Auditions, but please, make them more relevant to the daily lives of our students so that they want to keep on making music. So what did I do? I created my own Achievement Auditions at CMM, where students play three pieces of their choice, memorized.

The value of being able to play familiar music at a high level is immeasurable if we are measuring the longevity of interest in music learning. If a child (or adult) listens to classical music regularly, then by all means implement the baroque and classical music early on. Another idea would be to have a camp on this type of music and make it a rich and rewarding experience, but for the love of the children, we need to more wisely choose when to give this music.

Online Learning and Apps

The opportunities for online learning are incredible. I can't imagine teaching without an internet connection and an iPad. This is such an amazing time to be alive because of the amount, access and quality of information we have at our fingertips. Students love to listen and learn new songs using YouTube and the little ones really love Piano Maestro. Learning a song or two from Playground Sessions or the like is also fun. Incorporating a few minutes a week of purposeful technology makes lessons relevant and keeps the student interested, curious and looking for new projects.

If I were only allowed five apps to use in my teaching, here are my "can't live without" choices:

5 Essential Apps

- *GuitarTabs* for students who like to sing along as they play the chord changes.
- *PianoMaestro* for elementary students to learn familiar and fun music to play along with tracks.
- *ForScore* for music reading on your iPad. This is by far my most used app!
- *SuperMetronomeGrooveBox* for backing beats with scales or pop tunes. Another favorite would be *iReal Pro*.
- *FlashNoteDerby* for students (young and old) learning their notes. Completely customizable.

I'm a practical technology user, so there aren't any of the just-for-fun apps on my lists, but there are plenty of those around to have fun with!

Flourish: Get your Ideas out! What are some of your big ideas? Write your own Table of Contents for a book idea you have, or better yet, create a series of three to five blog posts on areas you are passionate about. Don't like these? Find a periodical specific to your instrument and write an article for submission.

CHAPTER 3
PICK ME! IDENTITY AND VALUE PROPOSITION

1. Differentiation

2. Print Materials

3. Website

4. Social Media

5. Résumé

6. Bios

7. Newsletter

Differentiation

What makes you unique? Your value proposition in the market is where you articulate the promise of what you will deliver. Your brand is your name and what people think when you're not around. It's you, when you are not present. "I'm just a private teacher" you say? There are thousands of other private teachers, likely hundreds within a 20-mile radius if you are living in a metropolitan area, so why should people choose you? What makes you unique?

Here are two branding activities that will help you figure out how to market yourself. These sheets are also available at KristinYost.com for download.

brand development
questions

1. What 3 words would a long-time customer use to describe your lessons?

    • Are these words what you wanted to hear?

2. Would you follow your own Facebook studio or Twitter page?

3. When was the last time you had an outstanding consumer experience?

    • Does your company/studio offer those same type of "wow" experiences?

4. Do you spend time furthering your professionalism by reading and attending development classes?

5. Can you explain in less than 1 minute, your vision for your brand?

6. Can you explain in less than 15 seconds what your brand does to benefit your community?

7. What is the most important sentence you can leave with your clients?

 kristinyost.com • kristin@centremm.org

kristin yost

branding worksheet

1. If you had to list your 3 greatest strengths, what would they be?
   1.
   2.
   3.

2. Is your personal brand a collection of your strengths?

3. If you surveyed your "favorite 5" students and families, would they say your strengths are those listed above? If not, what do you think they would say?

4. How are you communicating your strengths to your clients/families?

5. How could you improve that communication? (List 3 ways)
   1.
   2.
   3.

6. Is your website image reflective of what you want to be known for?

7. What does your studio space say about you? Is it an extension of your branding, or something completely different?

 kristinyost.com • kristin@centremm.org

Print materials

Believe it or not, it's still important you have print materials readily available, so I'm not ready to recommend throwing this expense out the window quite yet. Most people don't actually read the content of brochures, but you can grab their attention with a rack card, multifold business card and perhaps a unique business card. The point is, make it **memorable** so whatever you just spent money on to have a designed and printed advertising piece is not lost in the bottom of someone's purse or ends up straight in the recycling bin. Your energy should not be spent on designing this outside of content curation and initial ideas of what visual message you want to send. Hire a professional designer! More on that later.

Top 10 Essentials to Professionally Design and Print for your studio or school:

1. Rack Card or Brochure
2. Business Cards
3. Calendar
4. Posters for Recitals
5. Postcard for Marketing
6. Binder/Assignment Book Cover
7. Repertoire Lists
8. Top 10 Reasons to Study Music (with you)
9. Certificates
10. Awards

Extraordinary results in every student!

CENTRE FOR MUSICAL MINDS
9300 John Hickman Pkwy
Suite 405
Frisco, TX 75035

✉ INFO@CENTREMM.ORG

📱 214.586.4309

🏠 CENTREFORMUSICALMINDS.ORG

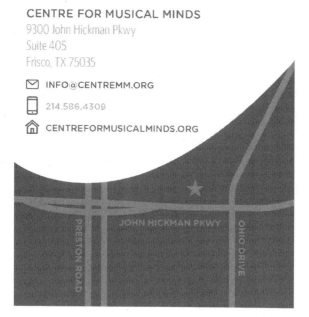

rack card example - front

$50 off semester tuition!
*NEW STUDENTS ONLY

CENTRE for MUSICAL MINDS

Classical to Pop and beyond!

- ○ **PRIVATE LESSONS**
  Piano, Guitar and Voice (in-person or online)

- ○ **GROUP PIANO LESSONS**
  Piano Safari! First time beginners 5+

- ○ **COMMERCIAL MUSIC**
  Songwriting and production

- ○ **UNIQUE PERFORMANCE OPPORTUNITIES**
  Retirement centers, concert halls and in-home concerts

- ○ **ROYAL CONSERVATORY OF MUSIC**
  Optional exams; international standards

CENTREFORMUSICALMINDS.ORG

rack card example - back

Website

At the moment, one of the most user-friendly and beautiful platforms I am aware of is Strikingly, though there are numerous options that are accessible and will work just fine. Your website platform needs to be easy to use. You are a musician, after all. It's not a good idea to spend your time trying to become a web programmer or designer. Whatever you choose to use, make sure it's easy for you to create, update and publish, otherwise you'll avoid it and your site will look disheveled.

This past year I moved my personal website over to Strikingly and have loved the experience with the final product. It's easy, beautiful and inexpensive. Strikingly truly makes things easy, streamlined and looks like a professional designer created it.

Fun fact: 85 percent of our website traffic now comes from Google searches. In order to have your site populate on Google, you need to be — and stay — relevant.

- Content must be relevant and high quality. This is the number one driver of your ranking. Use keywords, headlines, lists and bullets.

- Content must be updated regularly to show that you are an active site. Consider a blog or some practice tips that you are updating on a regular basis. Think monthly, at minimum.

- Have a link-worthy site with relevant referrals throughout your website. Suggestions might include your piano technician's company website, a link to your enrollment form or another website you recommend for buying instruments. Making your keywords bold can also be effective; just make sure not to overdo it.

The functionality of your website should be highly specialized.

- *Informational.* Meaningful and to the point.

- *Ease.* Streamline and simplify the enrollment process so that it's easy to enroll with you. We use a plugin from Studio Helper that streamlines and makes the process easy for the clients as well as us. There are plenty of great options out there.

- *Packages.* Again, make it easy. Offer packages for teaching and/or consulting.

- *Impactful.* Provide meaningful, relevant content.

Social Media

Based on almost ten years of experience, I'm going to share with you what has worked for my school. The highest engagements we have at CMM occur on Facebook, the most traffic to our website comes from Google, and Yelp is helpful though not integral to our clientele. That said, here are some helpful tips that can help you expand your social media presence:

1. **Be consistent:** this applies to your content as well as frequency. Post consistently, at the same time (schedule your posts) and vary the content, but keep it positive.

2. **Use multiple networks:** Twitter, LinkedIn, Facebook and Instagram are required but should not have the same message posted each day. It's important that you format for your audience, for each platform. LinkedIn doesn't need a daily post or a photo, and yet you need photos for Instagram. Twitter should be short, and Facebook should be concise and content driven. Posts can be different and still deliver the same message. One idea to streamline a bit is to have your Twitter and Facebook accounts linked, plan to post weekly to LinkedIn and take a fun photo a few times a week and use for Instagram. It is crucial to develop a plan/schedule and follow it for a few weeks to see how it does. Or if you really want to take things to another level, look at a social media management software like SproutSocial. It certainly streamlines and simplifies while measuring the impact of your posts across all mediums you are measuring.

3. **Push the platform that works well for you.** Mine is Facebook, so we run ads periodically. By periodically, I mean in a very calculated manner, approximately eight to ten times per year. Every time we run an online campaign we target the same demographics that we did for our mailer and work to be seen in multiple settings.

4. **Sometimes content won't be popular, but post it anyway.**

Testimonials are a great example, as are press features. You will get a few likes, but it's not like posting a puppy kissing your kid. Post them anyway to establish relevancy and validity in the market. You're building a foundation and this is a long-term play.

5. ***Amplify your business marketing efforts.*** Your social media plan is emphasizing your already laid-out marketing plan. If you are making it up as you go, take a step back and plan out a few months to a year at a time, with your tagline front and center, then grow from there.

Helpful hints: For content on Facebook, the most engagements come from meaningful posts. For example, the photos that feature specific children having a great experience seem to do the best. Focus on the ones where you are sharing a meaningful moment in time.

Here is an example of a two-week plan for posting to Facebook: research will tell you to post one to two times per day, and at specific times. Each social media platform is different, so user interaction on Facebook happens at specific times, in contrast to Instagram, Twitter or SnapChat, for instance.

The goal is optimum viewing, so we schedule posts on Facebook for 9:30 and 5:30 during the week, and 7 a.m. and 6 p.m. on the weekends. There are plenty of statistics out there, so do an internet search on social media and best times of day to post.

	WEEK 1	WEEK 2
MONDAY	Teacher's note and inspiring photo	Upcoming weekend event highlight
TUESDAY	Practice tip Tuesday	One of the top 10 reasons to study music
WEDNESDAY	Photo or 15- second video from teaching moment	Teacher's Note
THURSDAY	Cute kid making music video (external source)	Weekend event highlight reminder. Engage the community!
FRIDAY	Why Study Music related article or quote	Inspiring video from the news (doesn't have to be music)
SATURDAY	Free weekend event link from local news source. Engage the community	Funny (G-rated) joke and/or upcoming events at the studio
SUNDAY	Fun video that is not music related, but positive	Photo that promotes the studio or teacher

Social media two-week plan example

Social media image example 1

HIGHER STANDARDS MORE CREATIVITY

CENTRE for MUSICAL MINDS

Social media image example 2

Résumé

What's en vogue here changes from year to year. While most independent teaching artists don't regularly give their résumé to clients or potential clients, it is a good idea to always have an updated copy on hand. If you are applying for an academic position, you'll need something that is called a *curriculum vitae* (CV), which is a more elaborate and detailed version of your résumé. Please hire someone to professionally edit and proof your résumé. There is nothing worse than finding typos or misspelled words on someone's otherwise great résumé. There are some cool résumé apps out there that can help you find a great design, get you organized and won't cost you a fortune.

One of my favorite ways to stay updated and connect with clients is to have my LinkedIn profile up to date. It's free, and why not? A lot of people use this service for their careers and like to connect using this platform. It may (or may not) lead to a music-related job, but it will likely lead to parents doing more research on the education and experience of their music teacher, which directly correlates to respect and elevates your level of professionalism. It's an online CV; using LinkedIn for a weekly social media post is a great way to stay relevant and connected in the professional world that extends beyond our small circle of colleagues and clients.

Bios

It's a great idea to have one full bio, and two or three shorter ones on hand that you can customize to your audience.

For editorial placements, organizations often require a thirty-five-word bio, whereas at a conference, they typically prefer seventy or more words. For an attention-grabbing bio, it should be on the shorter side, with a link to a full bio.

Staying on top of your CV, résumé and bios is imperative. It's incredibly easy to forget the amazing things we do on a regular basis. By adding a calendar reminder every three to four months (quarterly) to make sure you are staying up to date with your professional activities, it keeps you organized and, when it's time to submit your information, it's easy and stress free.

Newsletter

Your newsletter is your opportunity to shine and share all of the awesome things you are doing professionally, maybe even personally. It shows your *value* to current clients. This newsletter allows you to easily raise tuition without having to feel like you need to justify your professionalism. Most organizations send out a monthly newsletter around the first part of the month, but do whatever works for you. If the fifteenth is usually a better time for you, then set that as your publication date.

Flourish: Get your online presence together. Whether you do it yourself or you use a design service, get your personal brand out of your head and into the world. Check out Strikingly for website creation and Fiverr or 99Designs for reasonable design services. Better yet? Hire a friend or local professional. Remember, you're a musician, not a graphic artist. Spend your time focusing and improving on what you are already good at and let the other industry professionals do the same.

CHAPTER 4
ATTRACTING AND KEEPING STUDENTS

1. Attracting and Retaining

2. Communication

3. Experiment and Results

4. Lesson Planning

5. Bring-a-Friend Week Ideas

You're already successful. You are a natural learner and teacher with a growth mindset. So, what is the science behind attracting and keeping students? Contrary to popular belief, "if you build it they will come" doesn't really exist unless you live in a magical place with the most perfect alignment of stars. So, assuming you want to thrive personally and professionally, it's imperative to know what exactly needs to be done to attract and keep your best students.

What qualities do you need to be aware of in your teaching practice that will attract students? The most important element is authenticity. People are attracted to genuine authenticity. Be yourself. Do you, at your highest level.

1. *Credibility.* Do what you say and mean what you say. Be transparent, kind and honest. This means you have integrity in your work and relationships.

2. *Marketing.* Your personality is likely the most important part, followed by credentials, and then your message needs to be clear, inviting, concise and consistent. Your website, your personal teaching space, your waiting area and any materials you are putting out into the world are important. Make it meaningful.

3. *Presentation.* First impressions are everything. It's true — particularly if you are in a competitive market. *How you make people feel* will determine your enrollment. How you make people feel when they come to a studio event will also likely determine if your client stays or goes.

How to keep students is also fairly clear-cut. All of the policies and processes discussed here are imperative to the streamlining of your business, but client retention is more about knowing the person than it is about the streamlining of your processes. The processes are for your peace of mind and ease of running your business. Client retention is simply about being genuinely interested and invested in your students.

1. *Know your student.* The personal relationship with your student and his or her family is one that is rare and meaningful. It's important for us to know the personalities, goals and interests of our students in order to connect and guide each individual. (It's also important to set professional boundaries such as office hours, lesson, makeup and tuition policies.)

2. *Goals.* Have a vision of your student as an accomplished learner. Set attainable goals. Incorporate challenge pieces to represent ten percent of the journey, rather than ninety percent. People (young and old) need to feel like they are moving forward.

3. *Joy.* If it's not fun, I personally don't want to be a part of it. How do you demonstrate and facilitate joy in your studio? What do your students look forward to? How are you making them feel in your presence?

Communication

Evaluate the words you use in lessons. Evaluate your tone. What message are you reinforcing with yourself and your students?

There are multiple ways to say things. Angela Duckworth, in her book *Grit*, gives a few fantastic examples of the difference between fixed and growth mindsets. The first of each set undermines the growth mindset and grit, and the second promotes it.

1. You're a natural! I love that. (Fixed)
2. You're a learner, I love that! (Growth)

1. Well, at least you tried.
2. That didn't work. Let's talk about how you approached it and what might work better.

1. Great job! You're so talented.
2. Great job! What's one thing that could have been even better?

The bottom line is, we can all learn to learn. Duckworth uses a quote in her book *Grit: The Power of Passion and Perseverence*, attributed to James Baldwin, "Children have never been very good at listening to their elders, but they have never failed to imitate them." Imagine the impact you will have if you focus on communication that promotes growth and forward motion.

Experiment

From 2013 through 2016, I kept track of each one of my student's repertoire lists, comparable Royal Conservatory leveling, theory level (Theory Fundamentals or Just the Facts) and asked each student on a scale of one to ten how much they enjoy their piano lessons. What I found out was enlightening.

Based on what I learned, all elementary students within the first two years of music study who do not have a known learning challenge learned between thirty and forty pieces from their lesson book as well as performance pieces throughout the school year. I found it was also important for each student to have a minimum of three pieces performance-ready for family and friends to really feel pride with their music study. Their enjoyment level skyrockets with this.

Intermediate students that had a high level of enjoyment in lessons, who had the interest and goals of a hobby learner, completed somewhere between fifteen and twenty pieces throughout the school year. Any less and I believe the leveling would be too difficult, which directly correlates to the student's level of enjoyment, interest and continuation. These students loved the process and product of making music, mostly for fun.

Intermediate students with the interest and goals of a serious hobby or possible music career were more challenged, learned their music with greater detail and their lessons also included technique and theory. These students learned between ten and fifteen pieces per school year, in particular if they were taking a Royal Conservatory Exam. Overall, their sight-reading ability was stronger than the hobby learners, and therefore these students were able to tackle harder repertoire at a higher level, in the same amount of time. These students liked the discipline just as much as the journey.

Results

Elementary students: the magic number of pieces learned throughout the academic year was thirty. All students who achieved this number continued on to the next year and expressed a high level of interest in piano study.

Intermediate students: for this group, the hobby learners needed to have between fifteen and twenty pieces they could complete and the serious students had ten to fifteen."

Advanced students: if the student is working toward becoming a music major, the magic number is about ten pieces due to repertoire and audition requirements, though if they are playing more for themselves, the number is approximately ten to fifteen per academic year.

Most students enter the school year with an interest level of about five to six on a scale of one to ten, but those who learn more pieces ended on an interest level of eight or nine. The students who achieved less in terms of number of pieces finished had more of a waning interest level and were in music lessons because their parents were making them or it looked good on a college résumé.

You must have a plan! Lesson Planning for New Teachers

There could be a whole book on lesson planning. Let's consider this the abbreviated baseline version. First, determine if your student is a hobby learner, serious hobby or pre-professional. The majority of students will fall in the hobby or serious hobby track, in which case this is my best recommendation for lesson content breakdown.

- Theory 5%
- Popular tunes 20%
- Familiar Classical 20%
- Standard Repertoire 10-20%
- Finger Exercises/Technic 10%
- Teacher/Student Choice 25%

Next, make a list of each of your students and include the following information to start your planning process:

1. Which theory book should the student use?

2. Make a list of books you plan to use with each student for the academic year.

3. Which familiar classical pieces do you want your student to know?

4. Which standard repertoire pieces do you want your student to learn?

5. List out the pentascales/scales you'd like your student to learn during the academic year. What speeds and patterns will you use?

6. Make a list of the student's performances throughout the year, and include two to three pieces you see them enjoying and preparing for each performance.

Bring-A-Friend Week Idea: Fun and great for marketing (activities-based)!

*Friend should actually have participated in activity-based activities during the lesson.

Recommended book: *Pattern Play Book I* by Forest Kinney.

Elementary Student Activities (activities-based)

- Tapping along with student, OR you play something, and the kids tap/clap (musically, please) along

- Teacher plays music in different speeds while the kids march around in time to the beat

- Arm-swinging with big beats (teacher plus friend while student plays)

- Have friend be the teacher and provide what they liked about the music

- Improv activity that incorporates both student and friend (Music Tree has great ideas, Pattern Play Persia comes to mind, World Peace OR your own activity)

- Have student teach names of keys if their friend does not already know them

- Have student teach their friend a warm-up exercise or create a creepy Halloween sound

Intermediate Student Activities (mix of activities and feedback-based)

- Have friend describe the music they are hearing, using descriptive adjectives that imply tempo, loud or soft sounds, what a piece of art may look like if the piece/song were a visual representation, etc.

- Improv activity that incorporates both student and friend (*Pattern Play Book 1*, first exercise, as an example).

- Student teaches an easy piece to their friend (depends on experience of friend)

- Blues improv activity (do *not* go out of the 5-finger pattern) with basic chords or single note in LH

- If playing a pop song, have student teach their friend the (probably 3) bass notes (do *not* use 5ths unless they already play piano) and have friend play melody over top

- Have student teach their friend a 5-finger pattern warmup

Advanced Student Activities (feedback-based)

- Have friend describe the music they are hearing

- Make up a story or poem on the spot to go along with the piece

- Have friend describe what they like about the music. Ask

leading questions such as, "What was going through your mind when you were hearing this?"

- Have friend describe what their hands look like, and ask if body language matched the mood of the piece

- Improvise from Pattern Play

If playing a pop song, have student teach their friend the (probably 3) bass notes (*not* 5ths unless they already play piano) and have friend play melody over top.

CHAPTER 5
PROCESSES: GO FROM SURVIVING TO THRIVING

1. Organization

2. Policies

3. Lesson Planning

4. Studio Management/Hiring Other Teachers

5. Taxes

6. Marketing

ORGANIZATION
To-Do Lists

The more processes (automation) you have in place, the more you can focus on what you really want to be spending your time on. For getting organized, David Allen's book, *Getting Things Done*, is hard to beat. Most Type B personalities I know shy away from making and keeping lists. If you make only *one* list per day, make it after your day is finished, for the next day, before you go to sleep. If you have a next action list that includes your to-do's for the following day, and a big-picture list, my guess is that your anxiety level will decrease. I'm pretty tech savvy, but believe it or not, I have a paper planner that is broken down by hour. It's how I am able to visualize my days. I can't seem to remember to check my Google calendar as much as I would like, and I find the tactile act of using a writing device to actually mark it in on paper helps me remember, and ensures I do it correctly. Of course, if I don't have my paper calendar, I add it to my iCal and set a reminder. The key is to find what works for you, and set a reminder.

Next Action

There are two separate lists you should always have: Next Action and Big Ideas. Next-action items are items that you should ensure are taken care of within a few hours, and certainly within the time frame of the day. What works best for me is setting a time limit to a task and planning each one in a similar pattern. The next action items are, literally, "next" on your list. Get lost on Facebook? Set a timer for thirty minutes and work to develop the discipline to walk away.

Big Ideas

Big Ideas should be listed separately from your Next Action List because these are longer projects. The larger the project or idea, the more baby steps you need to list and act upon to achieve your goal. The key here is making sure you are reviewing and chipping away at your big ideas project list. Set a recurring event in your calendar where you review and reread your ideas weekly or biweekly to keep them on your radar.

Studio Policies

Policies are great. They help you think through your process of handling attendance, makeup lessons, payment and other things you find important. People may skim over your document, they may even read it, but please save yourself from the frustration of thinking your clients will remember it on the level you do. Busy parents will ask for a makeup lesson, even if you have a no makeup lesson policy spelled out. Assume your clients are busy; assume they read a bazillion emails from their kids' schools, activities and work on a daily basis. Parents are drowning in information, homework and policies. A simple reiteration or reminder is all that is needed.

Be proactive. It's a great idea to send your concisely worded one - or two-page policy document out annually and collect a signature to show that they have read and agree to your terms. You could easily set up a Google form, or JotForm (that's what we use) to electronically collect your signatures. I find it helpful to remind people of the absence/makeup policy at least once per quarter.

Here are the policies necessary to keeping your books, schedule and clients organized. Keep each section brief. How succinctly can you describe each item?

1. Attendance
2. Absence/Makeup Protocol
3. Annual Enrollment Fee
4. Payment
5. Calendar Expectations
6. Performances
7. Student/Parent/Teacher Expectations
8. Past Due Accounts
9. Lesson Termination
10. No Food/Drink

Payment and Tuition Collection

Earning a living and living life fully is about so much more than getting paid. That said, the getting paid portion of being an artist is essential to say the least, and doesn't need to be difficult. Streamline this as soon as possible.

Let's focus on getting paid, on time. It's a necessary part of our jobs, and we shouldn't be apologizing for charging for this. There are several ways to collect tuition. Notice I said tuition. Please do not refer to your livelihood as a monthly or weekly payment. This sets the wrong tone. It says you're an hourly service provider. It says your value is only measurable by the hour and if you don't use that time, then you don't need to pay for it.

Choosing your verbiage *intentionally* is imperative, and the word tuition assumes your work to be all encompassing, like you would expect from a place of higher education. Your experience has value, as does your time, education, attention to detail, planning events, etc.

Tuition collection should be easy. The process needs to be simple. A poverty mindset will tell you to not take credit cards because you "lose" about two percent on fees. Look at it as a convenience and a way to get paid faster. Don't want to take a hit on the fees side? I completely understand. Look at it as the cost of doing business, and build it into your tuition price. Set your tuition to assume people are paying with a credit card and offer a cash or check discount if you prefer. Seventy percent of our revenue last year was collected using PayPal, and I wouldn't change a thing. Here are some convenient payment platforms that are easy to use:

- **PayPal** seamlessly integrates with *Studio Helper* invoicing and tuition payments are transferred to your bank account within two business days.

- **Square** is a simple swipe and within two business days your money is in the bank.

- **Authorize.net** allows for automatic monthly charges.

- **Quickbooks** works seamlessly with bank deposits and ACH, though integrating with your CMS may be tricky. Freshbooks is another option.

- **Bank Checks** can be set up with the client to auto draft each month.

Another advantage of using PayPal and Authorize.net is that the two integrate into the *Studio Helper* system. Once the semester invoice is created, clients can make tuition installments each month, which are automatically recorded in *Studio Helper,* then the system sends a receipt to the client as well as notifies me of payment. I don't have to spend time recording, emailing, stamping, going to the bank or paying someone to do that.

Lesson Design

The month of July is special for me. It's a time where I can sit with a free and clear mind and plan for the year ahead. This is when I do the most research on new music as I prepare for a substantial order to keep music on hand for the fall semester.

When I was acquiring my tools for teaching, I did far more planning and review than I do now. The point is, the more we do, the more we develop our instinct and figure out what works. It's like adaptive cruise control. You program it yourself, set your limits and go, adjusting as the flow increases or decreases in speed. It's imperative we have a vision for our students that is congruent with their goals, capabilities and support systems.

For my personal organization, each student has his or her own folder in Evernote, with performance piece ideas that I have for each performance event, which I update regularly. I also include theory level, any requests the student may have and a list of the student's strengths along with one or two goals for improvement.

One way to keep track of weekly ideas is through an assignment sheet.

CENTRE FOR MUSICAL MINDS

ASSIGNMENT SHEET

date MM DD YEAR

TECHNIC

PERFORMANCE-READY PIECES

1

2

3

REPERTOIRE & NOTES

THEORY

PRACTICE TIME

M
T
W
R
F
S
S

Assignment sheet example (int/adv)

This allows the student, parents and teacher to remain on the exact same page for expectations.

Components of the assignment:

1. A student should ALWAYS have three pieces ready to play for friends and family at any given time.

2. The repertoire section indicates works in progress. These pieces should not all be challenge or stretch pieces. Maybe one of them can be, but the others should be attainable within a few weeks.

3. Technique/Technic simply means finger work to focus on agility, coordination and strength.

4. Theory: Make it not painful.

5. Progress/Time Tracker. It's important to get into a routine of tracking time spent at the instrument. If you are seeing sixty minutes seven days a week but Kristy still isn't able to play her assignment with ease, you need to reevaluate and check in with mom and dad.

To pass a piece from the assignment sheet onto the repertoire completion list, I require 85 percent, which would be a B average. Most students will rise to 90 percent or greater if they really like the piece/song they are playing. Every week to every other week, the student receives a new sheet, which is placed in the front of their assignment binder.

Another way to track progress is through a repertoire sheet that is placed in the back of the student's binder for ease in record keeping. Through several years of data tracking, my research indicates that there is a direct correlation to enjoyment, longevity in lessons and overall progress when the number of pieces being learned is high, in particular during the first few years of study. Below is a repertoire sheet that we use at CMM to keep track of pieces during the academic year for students who are within in their first two years of study. Students who are in their third year or more have fewer pieces, since the length of their music is extended and level of challenge is higher. Please note that summer lesson tracking is kept separately, and includes ten pieces: some to be relearned, some to be maintained and some new.

In summary, you are keeping track of the student's progress in three separate places; one is just for you in your Evernote folder (or something similar), while the second and third are readily accessible to the student and the student's family at all times by being in the binder.

	TITLE	STYLE	COMPLETION DATE
01			
02			
03			
04			
05			
06			
07			
08			
09			
10			
11			
12			
13			
14			
15			
16			
17			
18			
19			
20			
21			
22			
23			
24			
25			
26			
27			
28			
29			
30			

TEACHER

RCM LEVEL

GRADE

AGE

NAME

REPERTOIRE ACHIEVEMENTS - 30

Repertoire sheet example

Studio Management

In order to have a grasp on a professionally run studio and to give yourself some peace of mind through streamlined processes, you need to be using a (CMS) Content Management System, otherwise known as studio management software. They truly do make your life easier!

The Top Five reasons to subscribe to one of these services are:

- Record keeping is all in one place. This is important when building your business.

- Invoicing is streamlined and simplified.

- You can get paid faster and with greater ease.

- You look more professional.

- It's a huge time saver.

Music Teacher's Helper, Moosic Studio and My Music Staff are some of the more well-known music specific ones, though I would encourage you to do some research and see if they are a good fit, or if there is something else out there that you think would work better for you. I have used Studio Helper for nine years with great success.

Hiring Teachers

Some of you may be thinking about bringing on another teacher to help with the demand in your area. I did that too when I was first starting out, and it was great. I drew from people I knew were strong communicators and great at connecting with people, in particular, children.

The most important question to ask yourself when hiring a new teacher is, "Would I want to spend time away from work with this person?" It seems kind of crazy, right? If you think about it, it's really not. Especially if you consider that you are hiring someone to represent *you* and your business. In the United States, we have two options of hiring people:

as a contractor or as an employee. Most teachers who work for you full-time will be an employee. If you are providing training to them, they are an employee. If you are requiring them to come to meetings, they are an employee. If you are providing them with equipment to do their jobs, they are an employee. Have a talk with your CPA and an attorney to make sure you are following the law. When you have employees, you are responsible for filing employment taxes with the IRS versus simply providing a 1099 at the end of the year.

Your working relationships are extremely important. In order to attract and retain top talent, it's imperative to keep a few things in mind.

1. When you first hire a teacher as an employee, make sure you train that person thoroughly, so he or she feels equipped to fulfill the job responsibilities. A great place to find teachers is through college music and/or music education programs, churches and through your network of friends.

2. Ensure that communication is clear and concise and that *you* are organized in your vision, message and timeliness in delivery.

3. In your communications, always allow 48 to 72 hours for a task to be completed. If the task is involved, outline your expectations well in advance so that your teacher/employee knows what is expected and when. As an example, let's pretend you are requesting student information for a recital from one of your teachers, who happens to have 20 students. This information should be kept track of, right? It's not enough to assume. Demonstrate to the teacher how you expect the information to be tracked; this includes which format you expect it to be submitted, with examples, and make sure you have the performance date on the studio/school calendar, months in advance. Then, when you request the information 48 to 72 hours before your deadline, the teacher will be prepared.

4. Autonomy is necessary for your teachers.

5. It's imperative teachers feels like there are development and growth opportunities.

6. Meetings should be efficient, purposeful and inclusive of other's opinions. I assume you aren't wanting to go at it

alone, which is why you hired another teacher. Make sure the teacher feels valued.

7. Most musicians are skilled at their craft, but are lacking in communication and/or pedagogical principals required to be an effective teacher. As an employer, you can provide an employee handbook, teaching seminars, workshops, training in the methodology you want to be implemented, pay for parts of their certifications, conference workshops, etc.

8. Set up time to observe. Ideally this will be in person, or you could have the teaacher record a few specific segments such as introducing a new piece, technique assignment and a full lesson.

9. Send out surveys to the students who have had a few lessons with your new employee, and ask a few basic questions (no more than five). Possible questions might be, "On a scale of 1 to 5, (5 being the highest) how effective is Mr. Nicholas communicating with your child?" Or, "Is the repertoire chosen for your child relevant and inspiring? If not, what could Mr. Nicholas incorporate more of?"

10. Make sure you check in and see how things are going and offer your support.

What other gestures can you do to help your teachers thrive, rather than simply survive? It's important to me to always have a faculty gift ready the first day of lessons back to school, another gift for Thanksgiving, Christmas, Teacher Appreciation Week and their birthdays. Grand gestures are not necessary, but thoughtful gifts and cards are. It shows you care about them and appreciate their presence.

Do you recall the last time someone made you feel special in a professional setting? What was it like and is that something you could replicate with your teachers?

Taxes

You may think I have lost my mind, but I view taxes as a gift because having the money to pay them is. When you pay taxes, it means you are making money and have the means to financially support the community.

This is definitely an evolution in my thinking. Perhaps even a revolution in my thinking; it's a lot more peaceful in my head if I think of it in this way. So, go get yourself a CPA and don't try to do it yourself. They are experts in their field for a reason, and I think with as much skill that is necessary in other areas of our lives, this is not something to pursue unless you have a genuine passion for it.

Here are some additional tax-related concerns to be aware of, depending on your state, county and city, though they should not be taken as a complete list. (This is another reason you need to make sure you hire a CPA. Know your local and state issues.)

- Business property tax
- Employment taxes for employees
- Quarterly tax reports
- Franchise tax
- Income tax (some states)
- Federal taxes
- Property tax on your home
- Self-employment taxes

Marketing and Annual Events

Your marketing plan is your long-term plan to attract new students. There are cycles in this business and it would be a big mistake to not have a long-term plan in place to keep the students invested in your brand, even if you are full now. Start by streamlining your year with events that have a similar theme and occur at the same time during the year. It's a great idea to change up themes of course, or make adjustments, but overall a degree of consistency takes a lot of the guesswork out of what works, what is expected and gives parents and students an outline for understanding what they or their child will be doing.

Here are examples of what we do at CMM annually, with slight adjustments each year to keep things fresh. Changes in the schedule are always a little tricky, and there will be a few stragglers who struggle, but it's worth it.

- *October:* Fall Performance Class
- *October:* Bring-A-Friend Week
- *November:* Fall Performance Evaluation (one memorized piece/adjudicated event)
- *November:* Fall Performance
- *December:* Holiday House Concerts
- *February:* Spring Performance Class
- *February/March:* Pop Showcase
- *April:* CMM Grammy Awards
- *April:* Achievement Auditions (2-3 memorized pieces/ adjudicated event)
- *June-August:* Summer Enrichment Classes and Camps

Above all else, make each one of your events look like an opportunity nobody wants to miss!

2017-2018 CALENDAR

	2017
SEPTEMBER	• September 4th - Labor Day / No Lessons
OCTOBER	• October 17th-21st - *Performance Class* • October 22nd - *Community Outreach Opportunity* • October 27th and 29th - *Improv and Art: Fall Recitals*
NOVEMBER	• November 12th - *Fall Performance Evaluation (optional judged event)* • November 18th-24th - Thanksgiving / Fall Break / No Lessons • November 19th - *Optional Themed Recitals – Steinway Hall*
DECEMBER	• December 1st and 3rd - *Winter Recitals* • December 8th - *Community Outreach Opportunity* • December 18th – January 7th - Winter Break / No Lessons

	2018
JANUARY	• January 8th - Spring Semester Starts
FEBRUARY	• February 13th-17th - *Performance Class*
MARCH	• March 3rd and 4th - *Themed Spring Pop Showcases* • March 4th - 17th - Spring Break / No Lessons
APRIL	• April 8th - *Achievement Auditions* • April 12th-21st - *CMM Grammy's*
MAY	• May 8th - *Honors Recital* • May 12th - Last Day of Spring Semester

Calendar example

Grammy award example

Promotional flyer for event

Pop Showcase flyer example

CENTRE *for* MUSICAL MINDS

B I N G O

MEET and introduce yourself to 3 other CMM kids	ARRANGE or learn a piece/song by ear	ATTEND one of CMM's enrichment classes	PLAY for a retirement center or nursing home	LEARN a jazz standard
ATTEND a live music event	GIVE a compliment to another young musician	PLAY in a CMM recital	FINISH a theory book	PLAY a piece from the classical period
WRITE 250 or more words on what music means to you	PLAY a duet with another CMM or other music student	TEACH a parent or sibling how to play something you've learned	WRITE your own chord chart	CREATE a piece of art to go with one of your pieces
PLAY in a performance class	PARTICIPATE in a judged event	MEMORIZE a song or piece of music	WRITE your own song or composition	CREATE your own ending to a song

Complete this card and receive a CMM t-shirt or trucker hat!

BINGO card

The Mindset of a $100,000 Piano Teacher

Marketing Management Checklist

Marketing is your long-term sales strategy and in its simplest form, your plan for continually attracting new clients. Here is a list of actionable items necessary to keep you and your brand out front.

	Advertising Campaigns
	Social Media Campaigns
	Flyers and Program Design
	Web Presence and Content
	Teacher Highlights
	Student Highlights
	Video Editing
	Communication with Organizations and Businesses
	Studio Space Design
	Waiting Room Presentation
	Community Calendars
	Event Planning and Communication
	Events – day of shows
	Faculty Bios
	Website
	Newsletter
	Product Sales Tracking
	External Ad Sales
	Market Research
	Monitor Budgets
	New Client Sales

Postcard Campaign Example (front)

Flourish Make a list of all of the areas where you can streamline your teaching responsibilities and implement two to three of those processes in the coming year.

Flourish: Dream up a creative performance idea that engages students and/or your audience. Draw up a Day-of-Show Doc and get it on the calendar for the year ahead.

CHAPTER 6
MANAGING AND OWNING A MUSIC SCHOOL

Let's assume you have a waiting list and you see market potential in your area for a music school. This alone does *not* mean you should own a music school. Owning a music school changes your teaching hat to that of a business owner, which is drastically different than a teacher and requires a completely different skill set to be successful.

There is a beautiful, romantic idea of what owning a music school may look like as you think about how much money you "could" make, and the benefit you could have on your community. When I reflect on my first two years of owning and running the Centre for Musical Minds, I am reminded of how difficult it was to get the company off the ground in 2008. We were in a recession, but more importantly, I was new to running a business outside of my home. My learning curve included managing people, taxes, budgets, networking in my new community and marketing on a whole new and competitive level, to name a few. I didn't plan for the amount of time it would take for me to get a grasp on everything I had to do. It was exciting, it was challenging and it was scary at times. I remember shopping at the Dollar Store because I didn't have much extra cash, if any. I wasn't shopping there because I was being frugal. I was shopping there because I couldn't afford Walmart. Thankfully, that was only a short period of time and I was able to figure out cash flow, which you can see in the Enrollment Packet on CentreforMusicalMinds.org, where I outline the tuition calendar.

Owning a music school is not for the faint of heart. Owning a music school is like running a marathon for the first time. It's exciting at the beginning for the first several miles, then around mile ten it starts to get hard, and you still have a long way to go. You're starting to get a cramp here, a cramp there, you need a bathroom break and the next water stand is three miles ahead. You have some exciting points coming up, but it's hard. Then, before you knew it, you made it to mile fifteen! There are over ten miles more to go. Your muscles hurt. You are exhausted. You are going uphill, but every now and again there is a short downhill break. Then, you hit the wall. It's mile eighteen and you have eight to go. You feel like stopping. Keep telling yourself, "You can do this!" You've had challenges before. Now is not the time to give up. Show me that grit. Show me what perseverance and enjoying the process look like. All this hard work will pay off and you *will* finish.

It's . . . exhausting. While you're going through it, the challenge seems unattainable. You may ask yourself, "Why in the world did I want to do this in the first place?" After you finish though, you feel awesome, right? But when you own a music school, there is no finish line. You are consistently running up hills. New hills, familiar hills and hills you didn't know would show up. If you are in for the mental challenge, the hard work and switching from musician to business owner, let's keep exploring.

While there are some fantastic benefits, owning a music school is not for the faint of heart. You *must*:

1. Be a strong communicator
2. Have strong organizational skills
3. Be motivated to keep innovating, all the time

Realize that a music school is not a cash cow as some musicians (academics in particular) tend to think, especially on the front end. The cost of running a commercially based music school is significantly higher than a private in-home studio, and there is a volume factor that one needs to take into account. You also have to be educated on government policies as an employer, legalities of being a business owner, general experience with leasing a commercial property, and, most importantly, you have to be a respected leader to your faculty, clients and as the face of your company in the community. In the beginning, the biggest shock to me was how much people wanted *me*, and not any of the other teachers at the school. These prospective families who couldn't get on my schedule would rather go to another school or teacher than enroll in CMM. The branding, I realized, was not of a replicable model, but rather, I had branded myself.

A music school is not always the next logical step in the succession of one's career. If you are considering owning and operating a music school, ask yourself if you want to manage people, if you are comfortable and excited about forging new relationships in your community and if you are excited about managing larger amounts of money (money that comes in *and* goes out.) If you are, I encourage you to pursue this passion with a CPA and an attorney consultation or consider signing up for one of my consulting packages available at KristinYost.com, where you can purchase a series that takes you from studio to school with ease, confidence and clear direction.

Sometimes it's nice to dream up a new idea, which may include transitioning from studio to school. Speaking from personal experience, I find that most people run around seeking distraction. In writing this book, I was constantly distracted. I went out and bought a new car. I bought a new rug to put by the front door. I started to shop for clothes, after I had thrown out half my closet because I was committed to less. Distraction comes in all shapes, sizes and comes at any time if we aren't careful.

Distraction can be through music, TV, people — most of all, we seek things. Things to wear. Things to do. Things to fill the emptiness. Things to which we can attach meaning, significance and life. What most people want and need is a place of community that has purpose, order and meaning. This can be created through a music school of *your* creation; a place where discipline will become prized for what it is: the backbone of enterprise and action, of being what you are intentionally, instead of accidentally.[1] If you feel you are inspired by this idea, then you owe it to yourself to explore what running a music school looks like, or simply elevating what you are already doing at home.

1 Your People Strategy: The Revolution, p. 20. Graham, Michael Dennis.

CHAPTER 7
MULTIPLE REVENUE STREAMS

Think about your career as a path for building wealth. Wealthy people have more than one revenue stream, and so should you. It is my genuine belief that the best financial move any teaching artist can make for earning potential outside of the core organizational teaching house is to set up multiple revenue streams. This is imperative because you will always have money coming in. Here are some natural extensions of teaching that I do or am inspired to do, and you likely already are doing on some level.

1. Adjudicating
2. Presentations and workshops
3. Additional enrichment classes in your studio
4. Publish and sell music you arrange or compose
5. Buying and selling instruments
6. Consulting on your area of expertise
7. Playing gigs
8. Accompanying
9. Publishing relevant materials other teaching artists could use
10. Subbing or working as a church musician

A personal goal I have each year is to be able to max out a Roth IRA with non-teaching streams. The reason for this is because I want my teaching revenue to be used for living expenses, travel and separate savings, where these other streams are used for retirement and investing. This allows a more effective budgeting over the long term.

As industries change rapidly, having multiple streams also gives us more peace of mind. If one area is slow for a few months, there is no reason to panic, but rather provides an opportunity to pursue and work harder and smarter on another stream. There is an ebb and flow to artist income.

CHAPTER 8
FAILING FORWARD

You're going to fail. You're going to "get fired" by a student — it may even be a student you really enjoyed. You're going to fire clients, or rather send them on, and make others feel like they failed. It's part of living. It's part of growing. Most important, it's a huge part of personality development. How you handle failure is a far greater predictor of your character than how you handle winning.

Failing is a part of growing, and it's important to view failure in a positive light. I recently read an article about how a family each night at dinner talked about one way they failed that day, and how they would work to not have that particular failure happen again. I thought this was a brilliant idea! Focus on the failure, own it, reflect and move forward. That's growth. Grit, right there.

I'm going to share with you three stories of how I have failed forward in my career. The first has to do with when I opened CMM and how I was trying to get a business loan, specifically for operating costs. I wanted a financial cushion, even though I knew I could make it work on my own because I had copious amounts of students I was teaching on a regular basis.

I had a great business plan with financials built out for several years based on a modest growth rate. I had collateral, I had an established business and cash flow of six figures from the previous year. I dressed up, practiced my pitch and was rejected on three separate occasions, from three different banks, and three different men. They all thought it was "such a cute idea" and said, "Sweetie, we'd love to help you once you bring your dad in here to talk to us." After I got over my initial anger, I started calling banks and asking for female commercial bankers, of which there were none in North Texas. I kept doing my homework and educated myself on how to speak to bankers, what to ask for and kept on going. I knew what I wanted and wasn't afraid to keep pushing. Did you know Colonel Sanders of KFC was rejected over 1,000 times before someone bought his recipe? One thousand rejections. That puts things in a whole different perspective, doesn't it? Every time you figure out one way that doesn't work (that is, you fail), you are one step closer to figuring out what does work–success.

Another example of how I failed forward happened to me when I was a sophomore in college. I kept playing this recording over and over in my brain, "Memorization has never been a strength of mine." This of course was right before an upcoming performance, and I started learning the music later than I was comfortable with. I was playing the Chopin Bb Minor Scherzo and took it apart forward and back, slowly and in every way I knew how, but I just couldn't kick that loop in my head. I allowed fear to take over. I didn't tell myself that it was exciting, that it was going to be great and that I loved what I was playing. I told myself I was going to forget. I told myself I was going to fail. So, of course it fell apart and I was completely disheartened, mortified and ready to quit music altogether. I went and spoke with my professor about it and she encouraged me to pursue other things. I couldn't believe it. I needed some support, a story about how she wasn't perfect either, how she had a performance that was less than stellar or something that I could relate to, and for her to help me through this (one) performance, out of many,

many other great ones I had given. But maybe she was exactly what I needed. Maybe, just maybe, I needed someone to mirror my inner doubt, in order for me to stand up and say I'm stronger than I think I am.

I had an opportunity to demonstrate grit. Perseverence. Quitting music? You've got to be kidding me. That self-doubt talk should have been thrown out the window. This teacher retired after that year and I had the opportunity to study with someone who truly helped me. Dr. Patterson at The University of Wisconsin–Eau Claire was the exact person I needed in my life to help me through my imposter phenomenon, which I address in the next chapter.

My last example for the purpose of this book has to do with a "bad apple" advisor in graduate school who pushed me to continue to dig deeper and stand up for myself. Of course, this advisor thought I was being disrespectful and was unhappy that I wasn't following her rules rather than seeing that I was going deeper, but that's what was happening. I was finding my inner voice, leaning into my growth as a teacher, and it was going in the direction of impact, joy and creativity. I was getting grittier, and it felt good.

Have you ever had someone who was in a position of authority or someone with expertise that placed a negative value judgment on you or your work? Someone who made you doubt your value? That happened to me, and I am truly thankful. I was pushed to articulate at a much higher level, and earlier than I felt ready, my beliefs about music and piano teaching, music learning theory and educational/life philosophy, which happened to be quite different than hers. I wanted big ideas to make my own. She wanted me to replicate everything she did. I wanted to ask questions. She viewed my questions as doubting her authority. I wanted to grow. She wanted me to replicate. Get the drift? I wanted to find my voice, and she wanted me to copy hers.

At the time, I of course wasn't thankful, but then the experience taught me to be stronger, more thoughtful and intentional, and I became a stronger teacher. I came out of that experience with so much more of an understanding of what I knew to be my own personal truth; she couldn't take that away from me. I also knew my value and worth was so far beyond her comprehension and understanding that I was able to grow exponentially because I wasn't trying to impress or check a box. I was given an opportunity to realize my highest self at that time. Lesson: Your value does not decrease based on someone's inability to see your worth (Ziglar.com).

What are some ways you have failed forward?

__Flourish:__ List 5 ways you have failed forward in your life.

CHAPTER 9
IMPOSTER PHENOMENON

Imposter phenomenon is when high achievers are afraid they will be "found out." According to a Georgia State University study, over one-third of successful adults don't believe they deserve to be where they are. All artists are likely to have some level of self-doubt at times during their careers, especially as a performer. There was an article a few years back where Lady Gaga was talking about her insecurities and how she had to force herself out of bed one day, look in the mirror and tell herself, "What do I have to be afraid of? I'm mother ****** Lady Gaga!" The point is she had to make herself get out of bed and face her own fears of insecurity. Even this hard-working, incredible artist has to face her own fears.

Fear, excitement, anticipation and confidence all wrapped up into an upcoming show. It's a lot to process. Mel Robbins of *The Five Second Rule* talks in her book about being the most booked female speaker in 2016 in the United States, and she said that before every talk, she has the same intense feelings that one could describe as fear and anxiety, but she turns those feelings into excitement. Hundreds of talks later, and she still goes through it.

All of these feelings take us to a place of vulnerability, putting your hard work out there for the world to hear and see, and in turn being open to sometimes harsh criticism. In 1978, two clinical psychologists, Pauline

Clance and Suzanne Imes, discovered that many professional women felt like they were living a lie. They felt like the reason for their success was due to luck and they had incredible experiences of self-doubt. This isn't limited to women, certainly.

The great part about Imposter Phenomenon is that it isn't actually a clinical condition, but rather something that simply happens. It's a phenomenon, rather than a syndrome. Imposter Phenomenon is linked to people who have achieved success in their lives and careers and who have a perfectionist mentality. How can someone be perfect at everything, every time? There is an element of luck we all need to recognize is part of our success, but so much of our efforts and work ethic lead us to the place of being able to take advantage of that luck.

Here's another way to look at it. You've achieved success as a musician, then as a teaching artist, and now you are looking at possibly starting a school. Of course, you probably do have feelings of insecurity. It's also exciting and a great opportunity to figure out something new. Will your luck carry you through? No, but your grit can.

When one doesn't feel like they are achieving perfection consistently, this is where the "imposter" part comes into play. It's the idea that if you aren't achieving perfection all of the time, in everything, you aren't really achieving. This is where my Type B personality takes over and says "done is better than perfect." To me, this saying means that I have an idea and it's more important for me to get it out into the world than it is for me to hold onto it and make it perfect. Of course, there is quite a bit of criticism with this, but I am continually improving, so I am getting closer to getting things "perfect" before I put ideas and other information out there.

I used to think that if I just do it, somehow running a business would be easier, or at least I would become more comfortable. Unfortunately, much like a public performance, it's not. I'm still playing a part. I'm acting.

Just like when I'm performing on stage, I am, to a degree, acting. We call it stage presence, and it's a learned natural way of being, like one might train a monkey at the zoo to act a certain way when people show up.

So while the act of performance hasn't changed much, what has gotten easier is knowing what to expect. I know I am going to feel a significant amount of self-doubt, some fear, anxiety and a sliver of excitement running a business. When I finish a "sale" with a new client I would really like to work with, I have feelings of being on cloud nine. It's not unlike giving a strong performance for which I have done exceptional preparation. Skill and a little bit of luck work fantastically well together.

What I have found to be the best way to work through my own imposter phenomenon is to keep on keeping on. Just do it, if you will. Keep educating, keep growing, keep striving for better and implement more processes when machines can do a better job than I can. Keep writing, keep experiencing. Keep failing forward.

Process of Creating

The process of creating is one that if we are not careful, gets lost in our daily lives. How do you create each day? Personally, I go in and out of the process of creation. Owning a school, I am always creating something; from lesson plans to meetings, marketing, processes, lists and budgets. Some of it is inspiring and enjoyable, and some of it I would rather not be doing, ever. I still have to do it, though. As far as creating music, I've found that I love to sit and play, although I don't love to practice like I used to do. I find myself growing through new experiences, traveling and reading. That's okay, too. It's a different season of my life, and I'm loving it.

Each year I give a performance or play on a recital with our students. Thankfully, I still have opportunities to perform at conferences where

I speak, which provides a built-in opportunity for an audience of colleagues. I find more satisfaction when I play music from the classical canon, though I have pure joy when I am playing some of the popular music that I find catchy. I feel fulfilled playing both, not just one or the other.

Creating musical experiences, or any experience at all, is one that takes energy and puts us in a place to have feelings of vulnerability.

How do you experience things musically now that you are on your own without someone pushing you to go to concerts? Often we have teachers and take lessons simply because it's easier for someone to tell us what to do, how to do it and impose a deadline on us, than it is for us to be self-motivated and set our own goals. Creating our own opportunities is part of being a professional, part of being independent and certainly part of being growth-minded.

If you could describe an environment where you have feelings of strength, what would that look like? How can you put yourself in that environment regularly?

Flourish: Make a point to see/hear live music once each month for the next year. Already doing that? Try something new. Check out a musical, Broadway show or artistic event you never would have thought to attend before this challenge.

CHAPTER 10
WHAT'S NEXT?

I've spent a significant amount of time and energy wondering what's next.

If we are continually looking backward, how are we ever going to be able to move forward? The time is now for us to propel ourselves forward. We have so much rich information at our fingertips, and in this age of information, we have every advantage at our disposal. I can watch YouTube videos and learn just about anything. In fact, I have a big garden full of homegrown vegetables because of YouTube.

As I write this book, I am admittedly living the innovator's dilemma as I find my footing to go forward into my next endeavor. It's a little bit exciting, and a little bit scary. Will what's next for me be an extension of what I am already doing? Will my next big endeavor be a complete pivot from what I have done with CMM or will it be an evolutionary next step?

Will I build my own building? Will I franchise my school like I had thought to do eight years ago? Time will tell. It's an exciting time for me and I am intentionally leaning into my own struggle. There are lots of budgets and brainstorming sessions that need to happen and plenty of times where I don't want to do the hard work to get to the next level. What I know without a doubt, however, is that the way forward doesn't include spending time looking backward, or being comfortable. What about for you?

If time is our most limited resource, how will you spend yours? Will you spend it being frustrated and consumed on the issues that come up along the way, or will you be proactive and focus on the good? Will you keep the status quo or will you pursue your passions? Will you take the time now to set up your teaching practice for the long view? Personally, I plan to spend my time on the critical issues for my career, surrounding myself with the people I need to be successful, being around those with whom I want to spend time, and continuing on the path of growing and learning. I plan to thrive.

Most musicians pursue personal excellence through whatever instrument or medium they choose. Classically trained musicians are working on their interpretations and technical excellence in the same way that jazz musicians are pursuing new and creative ideas. Both are working methodically to reach new heights. This is one way to find fulfillment, but what happens when you have a nagging sensation that there is still something more you have to offer? It's up to you to explore what else is waiting for you.

There is an idea out there that says we are vessels and it's imperative for each human to realize his or her strength and calling — similar in thought to having a destiny. I feel so strongly that my purpose is to guide children (primarily) by helping them love themselves and enjoy their processes. As an extension, that's what I am doing with this book, for you, my colleagues.

How does a person start to work through this if you aren't completely certain? Make a list of things you are passionate about and that you enjoy spending your time doing. Start with fifty items and then cull it down to ten. Are you doing what you love? If you aren't, how can you encourage yourself to spend more time with and on the people and things that you love?

As servants and respected professionals (teachers) in our communities, at times it can be challenging being the collection agency, the friendly face and the expert. When I was in college and graduate school, nobody showed me how to write a business plan, or taught me to look outside of the protective academic walls where I had lived for seven years. I learned it was up to me to educate myself if I wanted to thrive as a teaching artist. So, I went outside the tower and worked with people who lived their lives as entrepreneurs, business owners and independent artists. If your goal isn't an office in the ivory tower, what can you do with your skill set? The possibilities are numerous. Finding your path requires deep work, but it's meaningful work.

Most recently, I have had to dig deep to successfully market what I value in a hyper-competitive environment with one of the most saturated music school environments I am aware of in the country. While I was trying to separate myself from my competition, there were periods of time when I wanted to give up and move to a secluded farm in South Dakota (oh wait, that was my childhood). Even though the community was small, there was still a strong good ole boys club and my own self-doubt. I was armed with education, some rich life experience and surrounded by fantastic people, but I will still making things up as I went. Then there were other days when I marveled at what I had accomplished and the quality of life I had reached at a relatively young age. We grew up poor and on a farm in South Dakota, over an hour from the nearest Wal-Mart. I had come a long way. The growth was big and it was fast. I am able to live comfortably, travel, donate each month to the charity of my choice and still have quiet time. For me, that's exactly what I want for my life.

It's not about the money, it's about passion for living and I find the more money I earn, the less I want to consume. The less I feel like I need. It's a great place to be, and it's far more peaceful than the alternative.

To those of you coming out of your college and university training, don't be afraid to make up your own rules. Guess what? *You* get to create your own life syllabus. *You* determine which classes you are going to take and what your grade will be. The year after graduate school was one of my toughest; I felt like it was a real struggle for me to get my footing on what was next. I knew I didn't want to continue on with a doctoral degree, but I didn't know what was next. What do you do without a syllabus and constant evaluation of self in a letter-grade metric sort of way? You generate your own ideas. You live your truth. Will you simply wait until someone tells you how valuable you are, or will *you* create that value?

I have spent too much of my life waiting on the approval of someone else. It's what a lot of academia promotes. Their intentions are good, but if taken too far, it can be detrimental. Suicide is the second leading cause of death among 20 to 24-year-olds. Let that sink in for a moment. There is a rise in what is known as "effortless perfection," which says it's not okay to struggle and make mistakes. *Wrong.* Make mistakes. That's how we learn.

I have failed so many times. I say that and I am truly thankful for all of those failures. It was one way of doing something incorrectly. Of course, nobody wants to be the one who is struggling while everyone else seems to have everything together. I promise, that's not the reality. This is where grit comes in, though. Fail forward. Fail fast. Fail often. If you are failing at something, that means you are putting forth effort. You already have skill, and skill plus effort equals achievement.

We don't need affirmation to know that we have value. Sometimes it's nice to hear approval from someone else, but that means we are giving our power away. That means you won't feel whole until you receive that

The Mindset of a $100,000 Piano Teacher

affirmation. The problem and danger with how we are trained through school is that we are conditioned to be afraid of making mistakes. I can't speak for your home life, but I can speak for what typically happens in academic settings in this country: students are conditioned to think in a linear way with a value system that says the more education, the more expertise — the more value you have. This is not the case. We *all* have value, regardless of education level, number of competition wins and the like. Your interest and lens may be different than your professors, parents or anyone else, but you are still the most valuable person in your life. Your thoughts, your actions and your beliefs make you uniquely you. That means that how you thrive may be different than how I thrive, or how someone else thinks you should thrive.

Final Words

I have given you a collection of my ideas through this book - of what I consider to be a productive and essential part of teaching artist development. In a workshop format, this would be a two-day event to get everything in. In a college class format, this is two semesters worth of work. Spend your time now working on three areas: reflection, communication and business skills. Most college professors have never had to support themselves outside of their student status and acadmic jobs. This is a problem when the professor lives in an altnerate reality of what being a professional musician actually means. The vision of musicians thriving in their lives, financially and otherwise, should not be a foreign concept or based on getting an academic position.

Most things start from a place of simplicity, move into the complicated and then back to the simple. I have included my best advice and my own experience based on a successful decade of owning and operating my music school. Use this as a roadmap for your own journey and then create your own itinerary.

Musicians and music teaching artists have a lot to learn outside of our core skill set in order to live self-sustaining and thriving careers. Who am I kidding? We all do, regardless of profession. We are all on a path, but which one will you choose? Which path will you set your students on? Will you choose the path that is rooted in autopilot and guessing, or one that is intentional, and rooted in continual growth and processes in order to truly thrive? Any successful independent artist and entrepreneur has gone through many struggles. All struggles that result in action will result in growth.

The processes you set in place, combined with the deep (hard) work, will set you on the path to thrive in your career as a musician. Be part of the change you wish you see in the world and use your passion and perseverance to live life fully on your terms.

If I were designing a course on living life fully as a teaching artist and professional musician, here is my required reading list.

Productivity

    Allen, David; *Getting Things Done.*

    Moran/Lennington; *The 12 Week Year*

    Pressfield, Steven; *The War of Art*

    Robbins, Mel; *The 5 Second Rule*

Business Must-Haves

    Gerber, Michael; *The E-Myth*

    Tracy, Brian; Marketing.

Educational Psychology

    Duckworth, Angela; *Grit: The Power of Passion and Perseverence*

    Dweck, Carol. *Mindset: The New Psychology of Success*

    Seligman, Martin; *Authentic Happiness*

    Seligman, Martin; *Learned Optimism: How to Change Your Mind and Your Life*

Music Teaching Philosophies

    Booth, Eric; *The Music Teaching Artist's Bible*

    Clark, Frances; *Questions and Answers*

    Duke, Robert; *The Intelligent Music Teacher*

About Kristin

In her mid-twenties, Kristin began a teaching path that was inspired by the traditional but propelled by the creative. She began trying to solve the puzzle of how to keep students interested in making music with a goal of keeping them involved in live music throughout their lifetime. Through almost a decade of research and hundreds of students, Kristin has achieved a formula for success not only for her students, but also for herself. She emphasizes joy, creativity and perseverance with long-view goals that focus on each person as a collection of strengths.

- Certified Teacher with The Royal Conservatory, 2016
- Nationally Certified Teacher of Music, 2006
- M.M. Piano Performance and Pedagogy Southern Methodist University, 2006
- B.A. University of Wisconsin–Eau Claire, 2004

Credits

Cover photo: Rejino Photography

Cover Design and Typography: Adrian Suarez

96498023R00052

Made in the USA
Columbia, SC
29 May 2018